Summary

of

Spygate
Dan Bongino

Conversation Starters

By Paul Adams
Book Habits

Tips for Using Conversation Starters:

EVERY GOOD BOOK CONTAINS A WORLD FAR DEEPER THAN the surface of its pages. Questions herein are designed to bring us beneath the surface of the page and invite us into the world that lives on. These questions can be used to:

- Foster a deeper understanding of the book
- Promote an atmosphere of discussion for groups
- Assist in the study of the book, either individually or corporately
- Explore unseen realms of the book as never seen before

Table of Contents

Introducing *Spygate*

Spygate: *The Attempted Sabotage of Donald J. Trump* is a book written by Dan Bongino, with D.C. McAllister and Matt Palumbo. The book shows how Trump's political detractors in and out of the United States attempted to sabotage him during the 2016 presidential campaign. The book enumerates and identifies the major players in the operation whose connections he traces and reveals. Various events are highlighted to show how the people hired by the Clinton campaign orchestrated their moves against Trump. Bongino claims his access to information partly comes through his former role as a secret service agent for the Obama administration. In the introduction, the authors say it is an abuse of power for secret service officers to contact innocent persons without evidence of a crime committed.

They claim that this is what happened to Trump's team. Obama secret service officials reportedly abused their power by making accusations to incriminate Trump during the campaign period. He cites quotes from journalist Sara Carter and House Representative Mark Meadows who separately made comments about the left's attempts to make Trump look guilty. Carter is quoted as saying Obama officials used unsubstantiated evidence to accuse Trump of collusion with the Russians. Meadows is likewise quoted as saying there is a coordinated effort between the FBI, the CIA and the White House. The authors then make their own judgment and say the scandal is complicated and it is not a simple story. They say there is "... no conspiracy theory— that's something we're not interested in pursuing. We don't think all the actors in this scandal gathered in a smoke-filled room and hatched a plot..." They say that each of the players had their own motivations that led to the creation of a "false narrative that almost caused Donald Trump to lose the election and continues to hound him in his presidency." The authors say they are writing the book in order to expose what really happened during the 2016 elections in order to establish "truth, justice, and...the American way."

Part One is entitled "Making of the Trump-Russia Collusion Narrative." The authors cite the names of Paul Manafort, Alexandra Chalupa, Serhiy Leschenko, Victor Pinchuk, George Papadopoulos, Joseph Misfud, Alexander Downer, and many others. They give the back stories and backgrounds of these people and tell how they are implicated in Clinton's campaign against Trump. Manafort is cited as a political consultant with questionable foreign interests including Russian connections. His work history with previous Republican presidential campaigns is outlined by the authors. Alexandra Chalupa is cited as a driving force in making Trump appear as a Russian colluder. She has a history of working with Democrats and served in the White

House under the Clinton administration. Part Two is entitled "The Investigations." It includes chapters on counterintelligence, stages of the investigation, CIA contributions, and profiles of Stefan Halper and Michael Flynn.

Part Three is entitled "The Real Story." It includes chapters on the Russian interference, Hillary Clinton and Barack Obama, Clinton's private server, British Intelligence, among others. The book ends with three appendices: Timeline, Media Leaks, and Charts of Connections. The book is dedicated to "all of the police-state Liberals, swamp-rat Republicans, and delusional Never-Trumpers. The authors write that without these people who abused their powers, the book would not have been written. These people accordingly showed the authors what can happen when their power is challenged. The book provides answers to questions that have been in the minds of Americans. It claims that the Obama administration assigned someone to the Trump quarters to spy for them. The Russians accordingly have links to a research group that was hired by the Democrats to investigate Trump's dealings and incriminates him. The FBI did not do their job and hired a private company instead to investigate allegations of hacking; the company is linked to the Obama administration and the DNC. The book further claims that British intelligence played a part in helping the Democrats to nail down Trump. Ukrainians allegedly played a part in promoting the view that the Russians and Trump colluded. The Clinton Foundation has connections with foreigners who spread the news about the Trump-Russia collusion. The book also looks into the motivations of the people who helped frame, Trump.

An Amazon review says the book exposes the activities of people who think of themselves first instead of promoting the welfare of American citizens. It says elections "are just for show like many trials in the old USSR." The review warns Americans of forces that "injure our Constitutional Republic." Another Amazon review says the book reveals "a sad tail (sic) of ambition, weak men, political operatives and hubris ridden bureaucrats."

It warns that America could become a state like that of "Solzhenitsyn's G.U.L.U.G (sic) type of Deep State government run by unaccountable political appointees and bureaucrats." Readers laud the book for reading like a spy thriller. The authors enable readers to understand the complex through "word pictures." It is accordingly readable and meticulous with its sources. The book cites many of its sources from leftist news organizations like "CNN, BLOOMBERG, DLSTE, YAHOO." It is accordingly hard to ignore because even if the left denies it, the facts and sources come from leftist media. A review by *Rolling Stone* says there is no evidence that the investigation on Trump regarding his Russian links is politically motivated. The reports cited by Trump are accordingly "bad-faith speculation from Fox News personalities." The review continues to say that nearly two years have passed and the FBI's investigation has resulted to the indictment of more than 20 individuals and businesses and "multiple key members of Trump's campaign have pled guilty and information suggesting criminality within Trump's campaign continues to emerge." *GQ's* review says Trump's tweets are popular regardless of their accuracy. Readers who are inclined to believe him will accept that whatever he claims about the Russians "might as well have been proven beyond a reasonable doubt."

Spygate is authored by Bongino who wrote the bestselling books *Life Inside the Bubble* and *Protecting the President.*

Discussion Questions

"Get Ready to Enter a New World"

Tip: Begin with questions dealing with broader issues to ensure ample time for quality discussions. Read through all discussion questions before engaging.

question 1

The authors say there is "... no conspiracy theory—that's something we're not interested in pursuing. We don't think all the actors in this scandal gathered in a smoke-filled room and hatched a plot..." They say that each of the players had their own motivations that led to the creation of a "false narrative that almost caused Donald Trump to lose the election and continues to hound him in his presidency." Why did they write the book? Why is it important to tell what they know?

question 2

In the introduction, the authors say it is an abuse of power for secret service officers to contact innocent persons without evidence of a crime committed. They claim that this is what happened to Trump's team. What did Obama's officials do? What are they guilty of?

~~~

question 3

Part One is entitled "Making of the Trump-Russia
Collusion Narrative. Who are among the players
identified by the authors? What do they have in
common?

~~~

~~~

question 4

Paul Manafort is cited as a political consultant with questionable foreign interests including Russian connections. How do the authors describe him?

~~~

question 5

Alexandra Chalupa is cited as a driving force in making Trump appear as a Russian colluder. She has a history of working with Democrats and served in the White House under the Clinton administration. What did she do to become a driving force?

~~~

question 6

Part Two is entitled "The Investigations." It includes chapters on counterintelligence, stages of the investigation, CIA contributions, and profile s of Stefan Halper and Michael Flynn. What information do you find significant in this part of the book? Why?

~~~

~~~

question 7

Part Two discusses the profiles of Stefan Halper and Michael Flynn. Who are these men? How important are they in the alleged Trump-Russia collusion?

~~~

~~~

question 8

Part Three is entitled "The Real Story." It includes chapters on the Russian interference, Hillary Clinton and Barack Obama, Clinton's private server, British Intelligence, among others. Which of these chapters do you find most interesting? Why?

~~~

~~~

question 9

The book ends with three appendices: Timeline, Media Leaks, and Charts of Connections. How important are these appendices? Which one do you find most helpful? Why?

~~~

~~~

question 10

The book is dedicated to "all of the police-state Liberals, swamp-rat Republicans, and delusional Never-Trumpers. Why do the authors dedicate the book to them?

~~~

question 11

The book provides answers to questions that have been in the minds of Americans. What question about the alleged collusion has been foremost in your mind? Is it answered by the book? How do the authors answer it?

~ ~ ~

question 12

The Russians accordingly have links to a research group that was hired by the Democrats to investigate Trump's dealings and incriminates him. What is this research group called? What did they do to frame Trump?

~~~

question 13

Readers laud the book for reading like a spy thriller.
Did you have a similar experience reading the
book? What makes it thrilling?

~~~

~~~

question 14

The book further claims that British intelligence played a part in helping the Democrats to nail down Trump. How did they do this? Why are they helping the Democrats?

~~~

~~~

question 15

The Clinton Foundation has connections with foreigners who spread the news about the Trump-Russia collusion. Who are these foreigners? What have they done to implicate Trump?

~~~

question 16

An Amazon review says the book exposes the activities of people who think of themselves first instead of promoting the welfare of American citizens. It says elections "are just for show like many trials in the old USSR." Do you agree that elections are just for show? What does the reviewer mean in alluding to the old USSR?

~ ~ ~

~ ~ ~

question 17

Another Amazon review says the book reveals "a sad tail (sic) of ambition, weak men, political operatives and hubris ridden bureaucrats." It warns that America could become a state like that of "Solzhenitsyn's G.U.L.U.G (sic) type of Deep State government run by unaccountable political appointees and bureaucrats." What does the review mean in alluding to "Solzhenitsyn's G.U.L.U.G (sic)"? Do you think the warning should be taken seriously? Why? Why not?

~ ~ ~

question 18

A Goodreads review lauds the authors for being readable and meticulous with its sources. The book cites many of its sources from leftist news organizations like "CNN, BLOOMBERG, DLSTE, YAHOO." It is accordingly hard to ignore because even if the left denies it, the facts and sources come from leftist media. What do you think about the left providing sources for the book?

~~~

question 19

A review by Rolling Stone says there is no evidence that the investigation on Trump regarding his Russian links is politically motivated. The reports cited by Trump are accordingly "bad-faith speculation from Fox News personalities." What does the review say about the FBI investigations? Do you agree? Why? Why not?

~~~

~ ~ ~

question 20

GQ's review says Trump's tweets are popular regardless of their accuracy. Readers who are inclined to believe him will accept that whatever he claims about the Russians "might as well have been proven beyond a reasonable doubt." Do you agree? Why? Why not?

~ ~ ~

Introducing the Author

Dan Bongino, a former US Secret Service special agent, served in the US Presidential Protection Division in 2006 starting with the presidency of George W. Bush. He continued to serve the Division when Barack Obama assumed the presidency in 2007. He served under the Obama presidency for four years and left the service in 2011 to run for Senator in Maryland. In 2013, he published his book *Life Inside the Bubble: Why a Top-Ranked Secret Service Agent Walked Away from It All,* an account of his 12 years as a secret agent including his stint as protector the US presidents Bush and Obama. The book was a *New*

York Times bestseller. The book also discussed Bongino's work as an investigator of federal crimes and his 2012 attempt to run for the position of Senator. Bongino revealed in interviews that he run for office as a result of his experience in protecting US presidents. He says he disagreed with Obama's political ideology. When asked if he would have continued to work in the secret service if Mitt Romney won instead of Obama, he said: "it wouldn't have kept me there, because my frustration with the way the government was running had been a long, ongoing process." He was with the New York Police Department before he joined the Secret Service. Among his first assignments was to protect Hillary Clinton during her Senate campaign. After failing to win a Senate seat in 2012, Bongino ran again in 2014 for a seat at the US House of Representatives, running against the incumbent John Delaney, a Democrat, for the Maryland 6th district. Bongino lost the race with a mere 20,5000 vote deficit. In 2016, Bongino expressed intentions to run for the US Senate representing the 19th congressional district of Florida. He placed third in the primary held in August.

His book *The Fight: A Secret Service Agent's Inside Account of Security Failings and the Political Machine* was released in 2016 and became another *New York Times* bestseller.

He hosts The Dan Bongino Show, a high-ranking podcast. Before coming out with his latest book,

Bongino had been quoted criticizing the investigation on Trump. He said it was "a total scam." Trump has cited Bongino in his tweets, saying the former secret service agent is lambasting former CIA head John Brennan by saying the man "has disgraced the entire Intelligence Community." Bongino has expressed opposition to Obamacare. He says it is a scandal and endangers Americans. Obama accordingly treats the government as a toy and they are inexperienced in handling it. It will be catastrophic for everybody, he thinks.

He says the Obama administration is "toxic" and uses the "government as a weapon exclusively to intimidate enemies." He compares it to the Clinton administration which he says did not use government as a weapon the way that the Obama administration did. He says "...it's like giving a kid a Bowie knife and saying, 'Have fun.' They accordingly have no experience and "have just gone wild." President Clinton's speeches were not toxic compared to Obama's, he said. With Obama, "you are not just his political enemy, you are his real enemy if you disagreed. I couldn't listen to it anymore."

He said that if he were to head the Secret Service Department, he would remove the investigative tasks assigned to them. He says this is something he will do "out of responsibility to the government at large and the taxpayers." He adds that the secret service agents are good investigators but they are overburdened. As a member of the organization Groundswell, he has assisted the group's efforts to fight against the leftists and their anti-conservative activities. He is known for his staunch pro-Trump comments.

His other bestseller is entitled *Protecting the President: An Inside Account of the Troubled Secret Service in an Era of Evolving Threats*

Denise C. McAllister is a journalist and a pro-life advocate. Based in Charlotte, NC, her work published by The Federalist and in outlets including Real Clear Politics, PJ Media, Ricochet, and Hot Air. She has guested on TV programs like Fox News, NPR, CNN, Sean Hannity Radio, Newsmax TV, BBC Radio, and many others. She authored the book *A Burning* and *Shining Light,* a story about David Brainerd's ministry.

She recently announced that she is taking a break from social media after being threatened with rape, death, and violence for tweeting pro-life statements. Her September 6 tweet that said pro-abortionists' "hysteria" is traced to their desire for irresponsible sex. She said, "women have flung themselves from the heights of being the world's civilizing force to the muck and mire of dehumanizing depravity."

Matt Palumbo is one of the founders of Unbiased America. He works with Bongino doing fact checks for Bongino's podcast. His published the book *The Conscience of a Young Conservative.*

Bonus Downloads
*Get Free Books with **Any Purchase** of Conversation Starters!*

Every purchase comes with a FREE download!

Add spice to any conversation
Never run out of things to say
Spend time with those you love

Fireside Questions

"What would you do?"

Tip: These questions can be a fun exercise as it spurs creativity among the readers by allowing alternate scene endings and "if this was you" questions.

~~~

question 21

In 2013, Bongino published his book Life Inside the Bubble: Why a Top-Ranked Secret Service Agent Walked Away from It All. What does the book discuss? Who are the major characters in his book?

~~~

~~~

question 22

He served under the Obama presidency for four years and left the service in 2011 to run for Senator in Maryland. Why did he decide to run for public office? What experience helped him make the decision?

~~~

question 23

He was with the New York Police Department before he joined the Secret Service. Among his first assignments was to protect Hillary Clinton during her Senate campaign. What does he say about serving the Clintons?

~ ~ ~

~~~

question 24

Bongino has expressed opposition to Obamacare. He says it is a scandal and endangers Americans. How does he view the Obama administration?

~~~

question 25

Denise C. McAllister is a journalist and a pro-life advocate. She recently announced that she is taking a break from social media after being threatened. What caused the threats against her??

question 26

Bongino claims his access to information partly comes through his former role as a secret service agent for the Obama administration. If he was not with the secret service, do you think he could have written the book? Is the book mainly hinged on his being a former secret service agent?

~~~

question 27

When asked if he would have continued to work in the secret service if Mitt Romney won instead of Obama, he said: "it wouldn't have kept me there, because my frustration with the way the government was running had been a long, ongoing process." If Romney did win and if he did work under Romney, how different would his political career be? Would he be a Republican still?

~~~

question 28

After failing to win a Senate seat in 2012, Bongino ran again in 2014 for a seat at the US House of Representatives, running against the incumbent John Delaney, a Democrat, for the Maryland 6th district. Bongino lost the race with a mere 20,5000 vote deficit. In 2016, Bongino expressed intentions to run for the US Senate representing the 19th congressional district of Florida. He placed third in the primary held in August. If he did not pursue a political career, do you think he would be a prominent media person today? Why? Why not?

~~~

question 29

The book is dedicated to "all of the police-state Liberals, swamp-rat Republicans, and delusional Never-Trumpers. The authors write that without these people who abused their powers, the book would not have been written. These people accordingly showed the authors what can happen when their power is challenged. If you are the author, to whom would you dedicate the book? Why?

~~~

~~~

question 30

The book ends with three appendices: Timeline, Media Leaks, and Charts of Connections. If you are the author what other sources of facts would you include in the book? Why?

~~~

Quiz Questions

"Ready to Announce the Winners?"

Tip: Create a leaderboard and track scores to see who gets the most correct answers. Winners required. Prizes optional.

~~~

quiz question 1

The authors say they are writing the book in order to expose what really happened during the 2016 elections in order to establish "truth, justice, and...the_____ way."

~~~

~~~

quiz question 2

_____ is cited as a political consultant with questionable foreign interests including Russian connections. His work history with previous Republican presidential campaigns is outlined by the authors.

~~~

quiz question 3

Part _____is entitled "The Real Story." It includes chapters on the Russian interference, Hillary Clinton and Barack Obama, Clinton's private server, British Intelligence, among others.

~~~

~~~

quiz question 4

True or False: Ukrainians allegedly played a part in promoting the view that the Russians and Trump colluded.

~~~

~~~

quiz question 5

True or False: The Clinton Foundation has connections with foreigners who spread the news about the Trump-Russia collusion.

~~~

quiz question 6

True or False: The book also looks into the motivations of the people who helped frame, Trump.

~~~

quiz question 7

True or False: The book is dedicated to the CIA.

~~~

quiz question 8

He served under the _____ presidency for four
years and left the service in 2011 to run for Senator
in Maryland.

quiz question 9

In 2013, he published his book _____, an account of his 12 years as a secret agent including his stint as protector the US presidents Bush and Obama.

quiz question 10

True or False: Among his first assignments as a secret service agent was to protect Hillary Clinton during her Senate campaign.

~~~

quiz question 11

True or False: Bongino has expressed opposition to Obamacare. He says it is a scandal and endangers Americans.

~~~

~~~

quiz question 12

True or False: Denise C. McAllister recently announced that she is taking a break from social media after being threatened with rape, death, and violence for tweeting pro-life statements.

~~~

Quiz Answers

1. American
2. Paul Manafort
3. Three
4. True
5. True
6. True
7. False
8. Obama
9. Life Inside the Bubble
10. True
11. True
12. True

Ways to Continue Your Reading

EVERY month, our team runs through a wide selection of books to pick the best titles for readers and reading groups, and promotes these titles to our thousands of readers – sometimes with free downloads, sale dates, and additional brochures.

[Click here to sign up for these benefits.](#)

If you have not yet read the original work or would like to read it again, you can purchase the original book here.

Bonus Downloads
Get Free Books with __Any Purchase__ of Conversation Starters!

Every purchase comes with a FREE download!

Add spice to any conversation
Never run out of things to say
Spend time with those you love

Get it Now

or Click Here.

Scan Your Phone

On the Next Page...

If you found this book helpful to your discussions and rate it a 4 or 5, please write us a review on the next page.

Any length would be fine but we'd appreciate hearing you more! We'd be very encouraged.

Till next time,

BookHabits

"Loving Books is Actually a Habit"

CPSIA information can be obtained
at www.ICGtesting.com
Printed in the USA
BVHW071733070219
539735BV00002B/320/P